Published by Creative Education
123 South Broad Street, Mankato, Minnesota 56001
Creative Education is an imprint of The Creative Company

Designed by Stephanie Blumenthal
Production Design by Sharon Stevenson/Envision

Photographs by Derek Fell

Library of Congress Cataloging-in-Publication Data

Fell, Derek.
Wildflowers/ by Derek Fell
p. cm. — (Let's Investigate)
Includes glossary and index
Summary: Describes the different kinds of wild flowers,
where they grow, and what efforts are being made
to protect this special part of nature.
ISBN 1-58341-001-5
1. Wild flowers—Juvenile literature. [1. Wild flowers.] I. Title. II. Series.
III. Series: Let's Investigate (Mankato, Minn.)
QK85.5.F44   1999
582.13—dc21   99-10177

First edition

2 4 6 8 9 7 5 3 1

WILDFLOWERS

DEREK FELL

Creative Education

FLOWER
STUMPS

In Oregon, the English foxglove is seeded by lumber companies onto clear-cut timberland to hide the ugly tree stumps until new trees can grow.

4

All garden plants are derived from wildflowers. Some are restricted to very small areas of the world. Certain species of African daisies, for example, are concentrated in pockets of mineral-rich soils within a semi-desert area of South Africa called Namaqualand. Others are widespread on every continent—such as the common reed—which is the most prolific plant species on earth. Many of the wildflowers featured in this book were native to North America hundreds of years ago.

Right, wildflowers called bird's eyes Opposite, field of wild common foxglove

FLOWER
INTRUDERS

Invasive plants are introduced wildflowers that overcome native populations. Some examples are Queen Anne's lace and purple loosestrife—both originating from Europe.

6

Right, dandelions
Below, Queen Anne's lace

KINDS OF WILDFLOWERS

When Europeans came to America they brought with them many seeds. They either brought them deliberately, as in the case of garden flowers (such as cornflowers), or accidentally as happened with weedy flowers (dandelions). These weedy flowers often travelled across the Atlantic Ocean as tiny seeds embedded in soil on a person's boots or **contaminants** in crop seeds. These, in turn, escaped into the wild so that it is sometimes difficult to determine what is a true *native* wildflower (one that grows in a place naturally) and what is an intruder or *introduced* wildflower (one that has come from another place).

7

FLOWER
F A C T

*The flowers of the wayside daylily, an **immigrant** from China, last only one day, but as many as 50 buds can prolong the flowering display for a month or more.*

**Left, orange daylily
Below, creeping phlox**

Examples of native wildflowers include the California poppy, the sunflower, and the black-eyed Susan. Examples of introduced wildflowers include the yellow flag iris, purple loosestrife, and wayside daylily. In the case of daylilies, we welcome these for their masses of trumpet-shaped orange flowers, but purple loosestrife has become a nuisance, taking over **wetlands** and crowding out more desirable native wildflower species.

FLOWER

SUNSHINE

Evening Primroses are prairie and desert wildflowers that close up during the night. As the sun rises they will open their folded leaves into a balloon shape, then, as the light strengthens, display them flat out like a cup.

FLOWER

FACT

*Many wildflower seeds enter a **dormant** period soon after they ripen and will not germinate unless subjected to freezing weather.*

Right, variety of trillium called white wake-robin Opposite, field of white evening primroses

WILDFLOWER HABITATS

Wildflowers grow in a diverse range of habitats. Sunflowers are widespread throughout the Great Plains states where they like to grow in sunny open grasslands. Trilliums prefer woodland where there is plenty of shade and organic matter in the soil to keep their roots moist. Avalanche lilies like **alpine** areas close to the snow line. California poppies and evening primroses can thrive in the desert.

FLOWER
FACT

Center, a meadow
Below, Venus fly trap
Opposite, Texas blue-bonnet

Some wildflowers are restricted to very specific areas. The amazing Venus fly trap, for exam-ple—which has devel-oped traps on the ends of its leaves to catch and digest insects—occurs naturally only in a small swampy area of coastal North Carolina. The swamp lacks natural nitrogen—something the plant needs to survive—so the fly trap simply adapted itself to supple-ment its nutrient needs. by capturing insects.

exas and California are famous for spectacular spring wildflower displays. Following winter rains, **annual** wildflowers such as bluebonnets and winecups will flower spectacularly within a brief spring period, covering thousands of acres. Wildflowers attract many different insect species, which in turn draw lower **predatory** animals such as bats and songbirds, which feed higher predatory animals such as eagles and mountain lions.

FLOWER
BLOOM

The Texas state flower is the bluebonnet—a type of lupine. It often blooms with orange Indian paintbrush, making one of the most spectacular wildflower displays in the world.

Right, water lilies
Above, New England asters

Some of the most beautiful wildflowers are **aquatic** plants, growing in swampy areas, such as the New Jersey Pine Barrens, an area of vast lakes covered with beautiful white fragrant water lilies.

WILD ABOUT WILDFLOWERS

There are many good reasons to grow wildflowers in a garden, but first you need to check with a local botanical garden or wildflower **preserve** to find out what wildflowers are best suited to your region. It's also possible to purchase ready-made wildflower mixtures, formulated for particular regions of the country, and containing seed of both annual types and **perennials.**

FLOWER
SALAD

The swamp mallow is a type of hardy hibiscus that has flowers up to 7 inches (17.8 cm) across in the wild. It has been **hybridized** *to produce flowers up to 12 inches (30.5 cm) across. They are edible and can be used as salad plates.*

Rose mallow

FLOWER

DRINK

*Some wildflowers are valued as **culinary** herbs. The leaves of beebalm, for example, are an ingredient in a gourmet tea called Earl Grey.*

Center, dame's rocket
Below, daisy

The easiest type of wildflower garden to grow is a wildflower meadow— or **prairie** garden. This usually involves scraping the soil surface to remove existing weed and grass growth, so the seeds you scatter have a chance to **germinate** in bare soil and establish themselves.

If you have a small area, you can dig up the entire site, but for a large field it's better to make islands of bare soil so the wildflowers create colonies within the existing meadow grasses. Be sure the wildflowers you grow in a meadow garden are recommended for sun, such as purple cone flowers and pink dame's rocket. A path through a wildflower meadow can easily be made with a lawn mower.

FLOWER
F O O D

Camas—or wild hyacinth—grow from a bulb like an onion that was a food staple of Indian tribes.

Common camass

FLOWER

REGROWTH

*Right, atamasco lilies
Above, trailing arbutus*

Awoodland wildflower garden can be a good location for a garden of shade-loving wildflowers. However, the soil beneath trees can be shallow and dry, so it may be necessary to cart in some compost or screened top-soil from a garden center and raise the soil depth using tree branches or stones. Woodland wildflower gardens are especially beautiful when you can include a fern-fringed pool and a stream, with a bridge and benches to admire the view and enjoy the cool environment on a hot day.

Bunchberry is a type of dogwood, but instead of growing up like a tree it grows flat across the ground, forming large colonies of white flowers on the woodland floor.

17

It is generally forbidden to collect wildflowers from the wild. But many wild-flower specialists provide wildflower seeds, and local wildflower preserves are usually good sources for plants raised from seed or cuttings.

Left, pink lady's slipper
Above, bunchberry

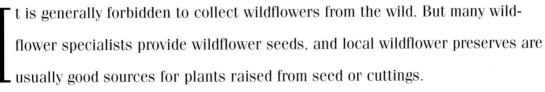

Wildflowers as art have been part of our culture for centuries—in embroidery, on porcelain, and on fine paintings, for example. The Japanese are especially skillful at capturing the beauty of delicate wildflowers on dinnerware, room screens, and fabrics. It's even possible to create long-lasting pressed flower designs using violets and primroses to create a colorful display under glass. There are inexpensive pressed flower kits available from hobby stores.

FLOWER
F A C T

About 50,000 kinds of wildflowers exist in North America.

19

*Opposite, mixed variety
Above, puccoon*

FLOWER

The famous Impressionist artist, Claude Monet, planted wildflowers in his garden because he liked their soft, somewhat imperfect appearance. These images were the models for many of his paintings.

**Right, wooly blue violet
Above, red Oriental
poppy among daisies**

Different varieties of wildflowers signify different emotions to create a special "Language of Flowers." Violets, for example, are "for remembrance," and a single violet laid between the pages of a greeting card is a way to add a romantic touch and express how much a person is missed.

Almost every country and state has a "national floral emblem"—usually a wildflower associated with that part of the world. France has the "fleur de lis"—a species of wild iris—as its floral emblem. South Africa has the protea, a large flower with papery petals that grows only along a narrow strip of coastal meadows near Cape Town.

FLOWER
F O O D

*The cardinal flower produces tubular red flowers containing **nectar**—an essential food of butterflies and hummingbirds.*

Left, wildflower meadow
Above, cardinal flowers

FLOWER

The California poppy is the state flower of California; it can cover hundreds of acres with its golden yellow flowers.

WILDFLOWER CONSERVATION

As the world's populations increase and land is converted to agriculture or industrial development, some wildflowers have become extinct and many more are endangered.

S ometimes the activities of people create an imbalance that upsets the natural world in indirect ways. For example, over-populations of deer—lacking natural predators and squeezed into shrinking wilderness areas—will **browse** a wildflower habitat so heavily that the plants are unable to recover. This is particularly true of native lilies and orchids, which deer seem to find especially tasty. Browsing by sheep and cattle, and **deforestation** also cause loss of wildflower habitat.

23

Opposite, California poppies
Center, lupines
Above, trumpet creeper

FLOWER

In New Zealand, the yellow California beach lupine—a beautiful wildflower protected in America—has become a pest.

Right, wildflower variety called baby rose Above, tree lupines

Even without loss of habitat, an introduced wildflower species can take over a particular area and crowd out less aggressive native species, which is why the multiflora rose (a **noxious** meadow bramble) and purple loosestrife (a rapidly-spreading bog plant) are now banned in many states.

Harvesting from the wild has also reduced wildflower populations. For example, European florists admire the wild pitcher plant that grows in southern swamps, and they have been paying farmers to harvest the plants, flying them to Holland by the plane-load for sale in exclusive florist shops.

FLOWER
FLEXIBILITY

The obedient plant—a wild member of the mint family—was given this name because its flower head can be twisted in any direction without breaking.

Right, Jack-in-the-Pulpit
Above, lupine

FLOWER

HEALTH

Purple coneflowers are the source of a product called echinacea which helps the body build resistance to diseases.

FLOWER

POISON

Daturas have trumpet-shaped flowers and prickly fruits that once poisoned soldiers camped near Jamestown, Virginia when they mistook the leaves for a type of spinach.

Echinacea

In other areas of the world, villagers are paid to harvest wildflower bulbs from wild populations—such as snowdrops, alpine daffodils, and dwarf irises—to be sold through commercial bulb catalogs.

A world without wildflowers would be a very sterile world, so communities that value their wildflowers often work to preserve a unique habitat by creating special wildflower preserves.

FLOWER
FAMILIES

Different kinds of wildflowers are known as species, and a collection of species forms a genus (family). For example, the swamp sunflower is a species of sunflower belonging to the composit family (commonly known as daisies).

Swamp sunflowers

One of the most spectacular preserves surrounds the slopes of Mount Rainier in Washington state, where thousands of acres of wildflowers clothe the slopes in spring and summer. South, along the Oregon coast, is another incredible preserve devoted entirely to saving the threatened cobra lily, an **insectivorous** swamp plant that lures insects down a long tube to digestive juices.

FLOWER
REBIRTH

If the pad of a prickly pear cactus is broken off it will form roots where the wound touches the soil.

FLOWER
NURSE

Many desert wild-flowers need a "nurse" plant in order for the seeds to germinate. The shade cast by the nurse plant breaks the sun's heat and prevents rapid loss of moisture.

Opposite, field of adder's tongue
Left, Oriental poppies

FLOWER
TRAVEL

The seeds of many North American wild-flowers are fitted with "parachutes" and are scattered by wind, sometimes for many miles.

Below, milkweed pods Right, ripe pods burst to release the seeds Opposite, sunflowers

The loss of a single wildflower species can have far-reaching effects in the world. For example, many insects rely on particular wildflowers for food. This is especially true of butterflies (the **larvae** of monarchs depend on milkweed for survival), and the loss of the host plant can threaten the butterfly's survival. The protection of land where wildflowers grow is important to our world. We must continue to appreciate all the color and fragrance that flowers on our prairies and countrysides have to offer.

Glossary

An **alpine** plant originates from mountainous regions.

An **annual** plant completes its life cycle in a year.

Aquatic plants live in water.

When animals **browse,** it means that they are feeding on wild grasses, plants, shrubs, and trees.

Wildflower seeds that mix with grain to become an unwanted weed in farmer's fields are **contaminants**.

The word **culinary** refers to something that is used in cooking.

Cutting or burning trees to destroy a forest is called **deforestation**. This may be done for any number of reasons, including the harvesting of lumber, the development of building property, or the creation of pasture for farm animals.

When a plant is **dormant**, it is resting and not growing.

When seeds first sprout, they **germinate.**

To **hybridize** plants is to cross two distinct species that do not normally mate in the wild. The new plant is called a hybrid.

If a plant was brought to one land from a foreign land, it is an **immigrant** plant.

Insectivorous plants catch and digest insects.

The **larvae** are the grub, worm, or caterpillar forms of some insects that will eventually change to become adult insects.

Nectar is sweet liquid made by flowers to attract pollinators.

Something that is **noxious** is unwanted, undesirable, and often life-threatening; some weeds are noxious.

Perennials are plants that need two years to mature and normally lives on from year to year without replanting.

A **prairie** is an expanse of grassland with wildflowers growing among the grasses.

Predatory animals hunt other, animals for their meat.

A **preserve** is a place where plants and animals are protected

Wetlands are boggy soils or areas of land covered with water.

Index